STOP THINKING OUTSIDE THE BOX

And 61 Other Lies You Must Unlearn

CHANNAN CARTER

Copyright © 2020 Channan Carter

All rights reserved. No part of this book may be reproduced, distributed or transmitted in any form or by any means, including photocopying, recording, or other electronic or mechanical methods, without prior written permission from the publisher. The intent of the author is to offer information of a general nature in an effort to help you on your quest of authentic living and spiritual wellbeing. Any advice or recommendations are made without guarantee on the part of the author or publisher. In the event you use any of the information in this book, the author and publisher assume no responsibility for your actions.

ISBN: 978-1-7349876-0-7

First published in 2020 by Channan Carter
California
Cover Design by Kostis Pavlou
In Collaboration with MacKenzie Thomas
Edited By Candace Johnson

@ChannanCarter
ChannanCarter.com

For my parents,
thank you for helping me discover my light &
encouraging me to chase after my dreams.

From the day you arrived, you've been programmed how to dream, what to think and how to act. As a result, you have likely not lived the life you came here to live but the one you've been expected to live ...

Today is the day you begin to change the program by unlearning the lies "they" instilled in you and take your power back!

YOU HAVE SO MUCH TO UNLEARN

UNLEARN:

THE HOW WHO
RULES THEY THEY
THEY TOLD TOLD YOU
TOLD YOU YOU TO TO
TO FOLLOW LIVE BE

SO YOU CAN BE WHO YOU ARE

DANCE LIKE ~~NO~~ EVERY ONE IS WATCHiNG

DANCE LiKE THE WORLD iS WATCHiNG!
DANCE LiKE iT iS THE SUPERBOWL HALFTiME SHOW
AND YOU ARE THE MAiN ACT!
SHOW THE WORLD YOUR MOVES!
LET THEM FEEL YOUR SPiRiT!
iNSPiRE THEM ALL TO GET OUT THERE
AND DANCE THEiR BEST DANCE TOO!

BE ~~CAREFUL~~ *precise in* WHAT YOU WISH FOR

WHAT YOU WISH FOR WILL MANIFEST INTO YOUR LIFE

THIS IS ONE OF YOUR SUPERPOWERS

INSTEAD OF BEING CAREFUL BE SPECIFIC AND DECISIVE

YOU ARE A CREATOR
WHAT DO YOU WANT TO CREATE?

~~FIND~~ YOUR LIFE'S PURPOSE

IS THE SAME AS EVERYONE ELSE'S

TO LIVE LIFE AS YOUR **AUTHENTIC SELF** NO LONGER LIVING THE LIFE OTHERS EXPECT FROM YOU. INSTEAD, HAVING THE COURAGE TO LIVE THE LIFE **YOU CAME HERE TO LIVE**

IF YOU WANT TO ACCOMPLISH MORE, DO ~~MORE~~ LESS

STAYING BUSY IS THE SHIELD YOU USE TO KEEP YOURSELF **DISTRACTED** FROM YOUR AUTHENTIC SELF

THE ONE CALLING YOU TO:

**FOLLOW YOUR HEART
TAKE THAT CHANCE • SHINE YOUR LIGHT
AND LIVE THE LIFE YOU CAME HERE TO LIVE**

YOUR MIND WILL SCREAM OUT EVERYTHING YOU MUST GET DONE
SIMPLY ANSWER BACK BUT FIRST YOU WILL DO THE THINGS THAT IGNITE YOUR SPIRIT

BEING CALLED CRAZY IS ~~BAD~~ *a compliment*

Working a job you don't like
waiting all week for Friday
drinking to forget the week
dreading Monday
caffeinating yourself to make it back to Friday
waiting for those two weeks off
is considered normal...

CRAZY IS A COMPLIMENT

YOU SHOULD NEVER HAVE YOUR LIFE FIGURED OUT ~~BY NOW~~

IT'S THE UPS AND DOWNS, U-TURNS, **SUCCESSES** AND OBSTACLES THAT MAKE LIFE AN AMAZING **ADVENTURE**. DON'T RUSH TO SETTLE DOWN AND FALL INTO A ROUTINE **BREAK OUT** OF YOUR COMFORT ZONE TRY LOTS OF THINGS GO LOTS OF PLACES AND NEVER STOP **EXPLORING** LIFE ISN'T MEANT TO BE FIGURED OUT SO STOP RUSHING TO GET TO THE DESTINATION & **ENJOY** THE JOURNEY

YOU SNOOZE YOU ~~LOSE~~ *Win*

THOSE WHO VALUE SLEEP ARE OFTEN LABELED

LAZY OR UNMOTIVATED

WHILE GETTING LITTLE SLEEP AND SELF-CAFFEINATING TO MAKE IT TILL 5:00 PM IS CONSIDERED NORMAL

STOP JUST MAKING IT THROUGH YOUR DAY RATHER, MAKE THE MOST OF YOUR DAY!

AND THAT STARTS WITH MAKING IT A PRIORITY TO GET A GOOD NIGHT'S SLEEP

I DON'T HAVE ~~SO MUCH~~ ANYTHING TO DO TODAY

YOU DON'T HAVE TO:

GO TO WORK • COOK DiNNER
WALK YOUR DOG • DO LAUNDRY
CLEAN THE HOUSE • WORK OUT...

YOU GET TO!

YOU'RE SO BLESSED TO HAVE FOOD TO COOK,
CLOTHES TO CLEAN, AND A JOB TO GO TO
YOU DON'T HAVE TO DO THOSE THiNGS, YOU GET TO!

STOP SAYing GOOD MORNING

SAY *great* Morning

STEP iT UP A LEVEL
RAiSE THE ViBRATiON

WHY SETTLE FOR GOOD WHEN YOU CAN HAVE GREAT?
START THE DAY BY SAYiNG GREAT MORNiNG TO THOSE
YOU SEE, AND END THE DAY WiTH GREAT NiGHT

~~DON'T~~ **BITE** OFF MORE THAN YOU CAN CHEW

TEST YOUR LIMITS
CHALLENGE YOURSELF
GET OUT OF YOUR COMFORT ZONE
TAKE RISKS
AND GIVE THIS LIFE YOUR BEST SHOT!

~~SOMETIMES~~

LOVE IS ~~NOT~~ ALWAYS ENOUGH

SELFISH LOVE IS NOT ENOUGH
THAT IS THE LOVE ONE GIVES TO GET SOMETHING IN RETURN:
SECURITY, STABILITY, WEALTH, LIFESTYLE, STATUS, COMFORT
BUT THAT IS **NOT** LOVE
LOVE DOESN'T TIE SOMEONE DOWN
IT SETS THEM FREE, IT'S FLUID, FORMLESS AND HAS NO CONDITIONS
LOVE IS THE MOST POWERFUL FORCE IN THE UNIVERSE
WHICH IS WHY...
IF IT ISN'T ENOUGH, IT ISN'T LOVE

SLOW AND STEADY DOESN'T WIN~~S~~ THE RACE

BECAUSE THERE iS **NO RACE** WE ARE ALL ON THE SAME TEAM

DON'T GET CAUGHT UP iN US AGAiNST THEM THEiR ViCTORiES ARE YOUR ViCTORiES

DO WHAT YOU CAME HERE TO DO AND CHEER ON THOSE DOiNG THE SAME

YOU CAN'T HAVE YOUR CAKE AND EAT IT TOO

DON'T BELIEVE THEM WHEN THEY SAY **YOU CANNOT HAVE IT ALL** YOU CAN AND WILL IF YOU HAVE THE COURAGE TO LIVE LIFE AS YOUR MOST **AUTHENTIC SELF** THIS IS THE SECRET TO LIVING THE LIFE OF **YOUR DREAMS** AND GETTING TO EAT YOUR CAKE TOO

YOU *never* GET SICK *ever*

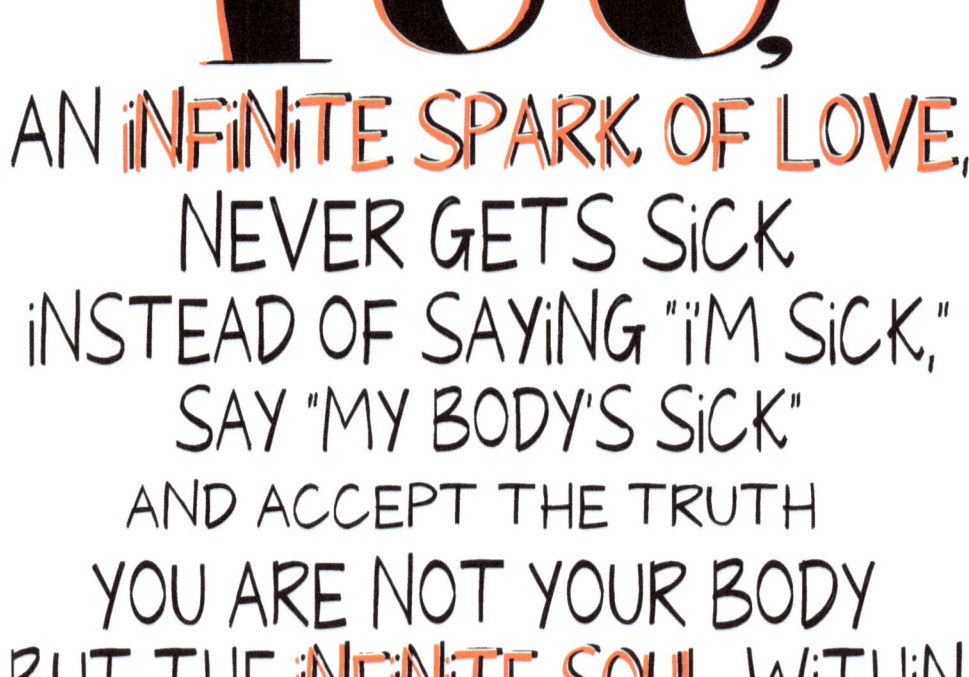

YOUR BODY GETS SICK
BUT YOU ARE NOT YOUR BODY
YOU,
AN iNFiNiTE SPARK OF LOVE,
NEVER GETS SICK
INSTEAD OF SAYiNG "i'M SiCK,"
SAY "MY BODY'S SiCK"
AND ACCEPT THE TRUTH
YOU ARE NOT YOUR BODY
BUT THE iNFiNiTE SOUL WiTHiN

TIME HEALS ~~ALL WOUNDS~~ NOTHING

YOU HAVE THE POWER TO HEAL ANYTHING & EVERYTHING YOU WANT

THIS IS ANOTHER ONE OF YOUR

SUPERPOWERS

DO NOT GIVE THIS POWER AWAY

THE CHOICE IS SIMPLE:

DO YOU WANT TO RELEASE THE PAIN, MOVE ON, AND REGAIN YOUR PEACE?
OR DO YOU PREFER THE DAILY ANGER, PAIN, AND FRUSTRATION?

HEAL YOURSELF BY TAKING BACK CONTROL OVER HOW YOU FEEL

DON'T
THINK ABOUT HOW TO SOLVE THE PROBLEM

QUIET YOUR MIND
GO FOR A WALK
LISTEN TO MUSIC
MEDITATE
AND ALLOW THE ANSWER
TO COME TO YOU

TAKE TIME OUTS
TAKE TIME OFF
TAKE VACATIONS
TAKE WALKS
TAKE BREAKS
TAKE TIME FOR YOURSELF
TAKE TIME TO RELAX
YOU MUST RECHARGE YOUR BATTERIES
BEFORE YOU CAN GIVE POWER TO OTHERS

THERE IS NO LIGHT AT THE END OF THE TUNNEL

the LIGHT

has always been within you!

FOR MOST PEOPLE IT TAKES A LONG JOURNEY IN A DARK PLACE TO DISCOVER THEIR

LIGHT

AND GAIN THE COURAGE TO LET IT SHINE

THE NEXT TIME YOU FIND YOURSELF IN A DARK PLACE: GET QUIET, SEARCH WITHIN, DISCOVER, CONNECT, AND TURN ON YOUR LIGHT

IN EVERY SITUATION
ASK YOURSELF
WHAT YOU ~~SHOULD DO~~
WANT TO DO!

NOT WHAT YOUR EGO WANTS
NOT WHAT "THEY" EXPECT FROM YOU
NOT WHAT YOUR EMOTIONS WANT
AND NOT WHAT YOU'VE BEEN TOLD TO DO
DO WHAT YOU WANT TO DO
THE THING YOUR HEART'S BEEN CALLING YOU TO DO
THE THING THAT SPEAKS TO YOUR SOUL
AND FEELS TRUE TO YOU

THERE ARE ~~NO~~ A LOT OF STUPID QUESTIONS

WE HAVE ALL HEARD THEM
WE HAVE ALL ASKED THEM
BUT BETTER TO ASK AND KNOW
THAN TO ALWAYS WONDER

SO ASK AWAY
AND NEVER STOP:

BEING CURIOUS
QUESTIONING
WONDERING, AND
EXPLORING THE UNKNOWN

DON'T JUST GO WITH THE FLOW

LiFE iS A BALANCE BETWEEN **FLOATING** AND **SWiMMiNG** THE KEY iS KNOWiNG WHEN TO DO WHAT SO DON'T JUST KEEP SWiMMiNG EiTHER!

FIT ~~IN~~ OUT

DON'T SACRIFICE YOUR SOUL'S DESIRES IN ORDER TO FIT IN

NO ONE CAN OFFER THE WORLD WHAT YOU HAVE TO OFFER

THIS IS ANOTHER ONE OF YOUR SUPERPOWERS

DON'T DENY THE WORLD YOUR MAGNIFICENCE

BE THE PERSON YOU CAME HERE TO BE

YOU ARE NOT BORED BECAUSE THERE IS NOTHING TO DO

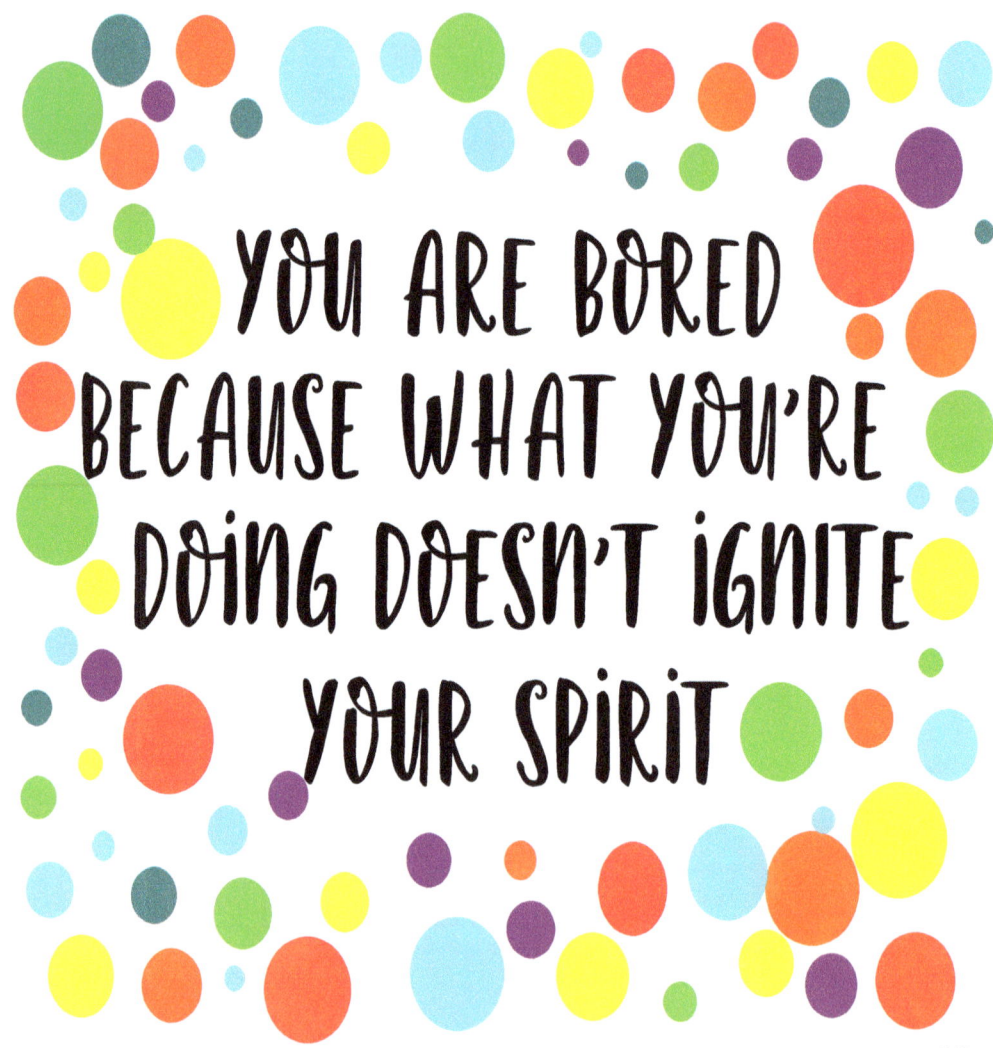

YOU ARE BLESSED IF ~~GETTING OLD~~ WHEN YOUR HAIR STARTS TURNING GRAY

FAR TOO MANY GREAT PEOPLE NEVER GOT THE CHANCE TO LIVE LONG ENOUGH TO SEE THEIR HAIR TURN GRAY

BE GRATEFUL FOR EVERY GRAY HAIR YOU ARE BLESSED TO SEE THIS DAY AND EVERY DAY AFTER

YOU CANNOT

~~YOU NEED TO~~

TAKE A LOOK AT YOURSELF IN THE MIRROR

BECAUSE YOU ARE NOT YOUR BODY
YOU ARE THE INFINITE
SPARK OF LOVE
OR "SOUL" WITHIN THE BODY

YOUR BODY IS SIMPLY YOUR
EARTH SUIT
WHICH ALLOWS YOU TO EXPERIENCE THIS MAGNIFICENT LIFE ON EARTH

YOU ~~CAN~~NOT WEAR WHITE AFTER LABOR DAY

YOU CAN ALSO WEAR:

SOCKS WITH SANDALS
BLUE WITH BLACK
MIXED PRINTS &
DENIM ON DENIM

EXPRESS YOUR MAGNIFICENT SELF ANY WAY YOU'D LIKE

THERE ARE NO RULES!

YOU SHOULDN'T CARE WHAT "THEY" THINK

WHEN THEY SAY YOU ARE STRANGE, DIFFERENT, CRAZY, LOST, WEIRD, OR AN UNREALISTIC DREAMER, THAT IS HOW YOU WILL KNOW YOU ARE DOING SOMETHING RIGHT

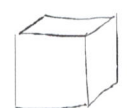

YOU'RE HERE TO LIVE AUTHENTICALLY, A LIFE TRUE TO YOU DON'T FALL INTO THE TRAP OF GROWING UP SETTLING DOWN AND WAITING TO RETIRE TO LIVE THE LIFE YOU WANT LIVE IT NOW! LIFE'S ALL ABOUT HAVING FUN DO THE THINGS THAT EXCITE, SCARE, AND CHALLENGE YOU THE THINGS YOUR SPIRIT CALLS YOU TO DON'T FALL INTO ROUTINE OR PREDICTABILITY BECAUSE THAT'S WHAT "GROWN-UPS" DO

~~NEVER~~ ALWAYS SURRENDER!

TO YOUR AUTHENTIC SELF
THE TRUE YOU
AND ALLOW THE
LOVE THAT YOU ARE
TO LIGHT UP THE WORLD

STOP THINKING OUTSIDE THE BOX

AND GET THE HECK OUT OF THE BOX!
DON'T JUST THiNK DiFFERENT
BE DiFFERENT!
BE WHO YOU ARE
NOT WHO "THEY" TOLD YOU TO BE &
ESCAPE FROM THE BOX!

DON'T MAKE A NEW YEAR'S RESOLUTION

MAKE A *New Day's Resolution* EVERY SINGLE DAY!

BECAUSE EACH MORNING IS A FRESH START, A REASON TO CELEBRATE, AND AN OPPORTUNITY TO MAKE A POSITIVE CHANGE IN YOUR LIFE

WHAT'S YOUR RESOLUTION FOR TODAY?

~~DON'T~~
COUNT YOUR CHICKENS BEFORE THEY HATCH

STOP BEING CAUTIOUS WITH YOUR EXPECTATIONS OF HOW IT WILL WORK OUT

GO ALL IN

AND

GIVE IT ALL YOU HAVE!

SEE THE CHICKENS
COUNT THE CHICKENS
NAME THE CHICKENS

EXPECT THINGS TO WORK OUT AND THEY WILL!

WHEN IN ROME, DON'T DO AS THE ROMANS

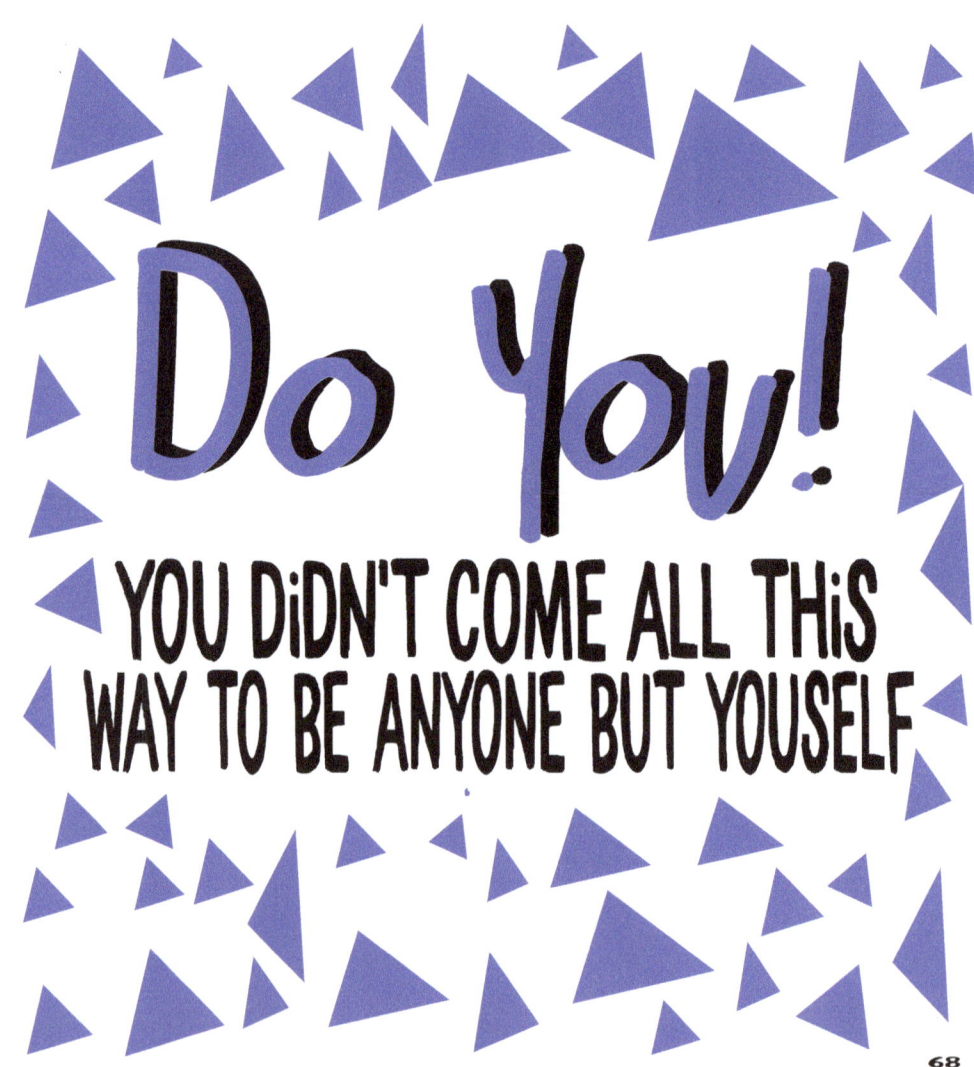

SELFISH PEOPLE DON'T LOVE THEMSELVES ENOUGH ~~TOO MUCH~~

WHICH IS WHY THEY FEEL THE NEED TO ACQUIRE
IT IS AN ATTEMPT TO FILL THE VOID WITHIN THEM

ONES WHO LOVE THEMSELVES ARE ALREADY WHOLE AND THEREFORE FREE

SELF LOVE IS NOT A SELFISH ACT
SELF LOVE IS THE MOST IMPORTANT SKILL YOU CAN LEARN

IT IS THE KEY TO LIVING LIFE AUTHENTICALLY
AND MANIFESTING YOUR DREAMS INTO REALITY

EVEN IF YOU GO OUTSIDE WITHOUT YOUR JACKET, YOU WILL NEVER CATCH A COLD

YOU CAN ONLY GET A COLD BY COMING IN CONTACT WITH A VIRUS... SO NO MORE EXCUSES!

go outside in the rain

SPLASH IN THOSE PUDDLES

dance with the raindrops

PLAY FOOTBALL WITH FRIENDS

go for a long walk

DO WHATEVER YOUR SPIRIT CALLS YOU TO DO! THEN WASH YOUR HANDS AFTERWARD!

NO ONE IS ~~PERFECT~~ *you are* PERFECT

YOU ARE *perfectly* YOU!

THERE ARE 7,530,000,000 PEOPLE iN THE WORLD, AND NONE OF THEM ARE LiKE YOU!

be you; you're perfect!

STICKS AND STONES MAY BREAK SOMEONE'S BONES, BUT WORDS CAN DESTROY ~~NEVER HURT~~ THEM

YOUR WORDS HAVE AN IMPACT ON ALL WHO HEAR THEM
THIS IS ANOTHER ONE OF YOUR

SUPERPOWERS

AND THE ONE THAT CARRIES THE MOST RESPONSIBILITY

IT MAY TAKE TWO SECONDS TO SAY IT
BUT IT MAY STAY WITH THEM FOREVER
SO BE THOUGHTFUL IN WHAT YOU SAY

IN EVERY CONVERSATION YOU HAVE THE OPPORTUNITY
TO BUILD THEM UP OR BRING THEM DOWN

BE THE SUPERHERO THAT YOU ARE

AND RAISE THE ENERGY OF THOSE AROUND YOU WITH A
SIMPLE COMMENT OR COMPLIMENT

YOUR WORDS HAVE THE POWER TO

CHANGE LIVES

HOW WILL YOU USE YOUR POWER TODAY?

~~DON'T~~ GET YOUR SHOES AS DIRTY AS POSSIBLE

STOP TIPTOEING THROUGH LiFE AFRAiD TO GET YOUR SHOES DIRTY

SHOES COME AND GO SOME OPPORTUNITIES ONLY COME AROUND ONCE

~~IS~~ THE GLASS IS NOT HALF EMPTY OR HALF FULL~~?~~

A HALF FULL OR EMPTY GLASS IS FULL OF POTENTIAL

A HALF-FULL GLASS OF SODA HAS THE POTENTIAL TO BECOME THE WORLD'S BEST COCKTAIL

A HALF-EMPTY GLASS OF MILK HAS THE POTENTIAL TO BECOME A DELICIOUS MILKSHAKE

A HALF-FULL GLASS OF WATER HAS THE POTENTIAL TO COOL YOU OFF BY THROWING IT ON YOUR FACE

MUCH LIKE THE GLASS, YOUR DAY IS FULL OF POTENTIAL

THE QUESTION IS WHAT ARE YOU GOING TO MAKE OF IT?

DON'T
FIND TIME TO:
MEDITATE,
DESTRESS,
BREATHE,
RELAX,
EXERCISE,
WATCH SUNSETS

MAKE THE TIME!

STOP TELLING YOURSELF YOU DON'T HAVE TIME WHEN THE TRUTH IS, IT JUST ISN'T A PRIORITY TO YOU

YOU FOUND TIME TO EAT TODAY, RIGHT? SLEEP? WATCH TV? CHECK YOUR SOCIALS?

BUT HOW MUCH TIME DID YOU SPEND ON YOURSELF? YOU MUST MAKE YOURSELF FIRST PRIORITY!

WHAT WILL YOU MAKE TIME FOR TODAY?

HARD WORK DOESN'T PAY~~S~~ OFF

Smart work does!

WORKING HARD DOES NOT GURANTEE SUCCESS
BUT WORKING SMART DOES
AND THE SMARTEST WORK YOU'LL EVER DO
IS WORKING TO IMPROVE YOURSELF!

~~DON'T~~ PUT
ALL YOUR EGGS
IN ONE BASKET

PUT ALL YOUR "EGGS"
(YOUR ENERGY AND EFFORT)
INTO LIVING LIFE AS YOUR
AUTHENTIC SELF

EVEN IF IT AIN'T BROKE, ~~DON'T~~ FIX IT

Everything can get better!

TOO MANY PEOPLE WAIT FOR DARKNESS & STRUGGLE TO MAKE A POSITIVE CHANGE IN THEIR LIVES BUT YOU HAVE INFINITE ABILITIES TO GROW!

So stop waiting till it is broken to improve it!

CHASE YOUR DREAMS • TAKE RISKS
BE OPEN TO CHANGE
STRIVE TO GET BETTER DAILY
STOP SETTLING FOR GOOD ENOUGH
AND NEVER CEASE YOUR EXPLORATION FOR SELF-IMPROVEMENT!

IT'S NEVER TOO LATE TO ...

Do anything you want to do EVER!

so what are you waiting for?

START THAT BUSINESS • SING THAT SONG
GO ALL IN • TELL THEM YOU LOVE THEM
VISIT THAT PLACE • CHASE THAT DREAM
TELL YOUR STORY • TAKE THAT CHANCE

SANTA CLAUS IS NOT REAL

SANTA ISN'T AN OLD MAN WITH MAGICAL REINDEER, BUT A MAGICAL SPIRIT THAT EMBODIES MILLIONS OF GRANDMAS, COWORKERS, AND OTHER ORDINARY PEOPLE FOR A WEEK A YEAR TO GIVE TO THOSE PEOPLE WHO ARE SPECIAL IN THEIR LIVES

THEIR **PERCEPTION IS** ~~REALITY~~
NOT A REFLECTION OF YOU

it's a reflection of them!

YOU CAN LEARN A LOT ABOUT
OTHERS BY OBSERVING WHAT
THEY CHOOSE TO SEE IN YOU

FORGIVE ~~BUT~~ AND ~~NEVER~~ FORGET

Forget it all!
WIPE THE SLATE CLEAN AND START NEW EACH DAY

YOUR PROGRAMMED MIND IS SCREAMING:

But what if it happens again?

THEN YOU DIDN'T LEARN FROM THE SITUATION THE FIRST TIME

LEARN FROM THE SITUATION • GROW FROM IT
BE GRATEFUL FOR THE PERSON YOU'VE BECOME
AND LET GO OF THE PAIN THAT GOT YOU THERE

YOU ARE NOT "x" YEARS OLD

YOUR "AGE" IS SIMPLY THE NUMBER OF TIMES YOUR BODY HAS TRAVELED AROUND THE SUN

STOP ALLOWING THIS NUMBER TO DICTATE WHAT YOU SHOULD BE DOING IN YOUR LIFE OR HOW YOU SHOULD ACT

DO THINGS ON YOUR TIME AND NOT BECAUSE IT IS WHAT IS EXPECTED OF PEOPLE AT YOUR AGE

AND ABOVE ALL, NEVER GROW TOO OLD FOR THE THINGS YOU LOVE!

Your soul is infinite your earth age is irrelevant

NO ONE ~~THEY~~ CAN ANNOY ME

AND WHEN THEY DO, IT IS BECAUSE YOU ALLOW THEM TO!

YOU CONTROL HOW YOU FEEL!

THIS IS ANOTHER ONE OF YOUR **SUPERPOWERS**

DON'T GIVE THIS POWER TO OTHERS

THE NEXT TIME SOMEONE "ANNOYS" YOU, TAKE YOUR POWER BACK AND ASK YOURSELF IS THIS HOW I WANT TO ALLOW MYSELF TO FEEL?

STOP TRYING TO CONTROL YOUR THOUGHTS

THE KEY IS TO STOP LETTING YOUR THOUGHTS **CONTROL YOU!** YOU ARE **NOT** YOUR THOUGHTS! DO NOT BE A VICTIM TO THE DAILY **CHATTER**! **STOP ENGAGING** WITH THOSE THOUGHTS OF DOUBT, FEAR, WORRY, STRESS, AND ANGER! **STOP BELIEVING** THOUGHTS THAT YOU ARE NOT SMART, PRETTY, OR CAPABLE ENOUGH TO MAKE IT HAPPEN! **STOP BEING YOUR BIGGEST CRITIC!** SIMPLY **OBSERVE** YOUR THOUGHTS **RELEASE** THE ONES THAT DO NOT SERVE YOU, AND **HOLD ON** TO THOSE THAT DO!

NEVER FAKE IT TILL YOU MAKE IT!

YOU DID NOT COME ALL THIS WAY
TO BE ANYONE BUT YOUR TRUE SELF

BE WHO YOU CAME TO BE
REGARDLESS WHAT THEY MAY SAY

FIND WHAT SETS YOUR SOUL ON
fire
AND GO ALL IN ON IT!

NEVER FAKE IT TILL YOU MAKE IT
BELIEVE IT, SEE IT, FEEL IT
AND YOU WILL ACHIEVE IT

~~NEVER~~ GIVE UP!

GIVE UP:

THE PRESSURE OF TRYING TO BE PERFECT
WORRYING ABOUT TOMORROW
YOUR DOUBTS   PEOPLE PLEASING
NEGATIVE SELF-TALK   OVERTHINKING
BEING WHO "THEY" TOLD YOU TO BE
ANGER FROM THE PAST   STRESS
COMPARING YOURSELF TO OTHERS
YOUR FEAR OF LIVING AUTHENTICALLY
GMOS   TOXIC RELATIONSHIPS
WORRYING ABOUT WHAT OTHERS THINK

EVERY WAR EVER FOUGHT HAS BEEN A CIVIL WAR

WARS FOUGHT BETWEEN
CITIZENS OF EARTH
BROTHERS AND SISTERS OF THE UNIVERSE

INVISIBLE BOUNDARIES AND FLAGS ARE THERE TO CONVINCE US WE ARE DIFFERENT, BUT

WE ARE ALL ONE

TEMPORARY INHABITANTS OF THIS BEAUTIFUL FLYING ROCK WE CALL EARTH
INFINITE RESIDENTS OF THIS EVER EXPANDING UNIVERSE

YOU WILL EXPERIENCE ~~MANY~~ NO OBSTACLES IN YOUR LIFE Zero!

ONLY OPPORTUNITIES
TO LEARN, GROW, AND BECOME BETTER

EMBRACE THESE OPPORTUNITIES
BE OPEN TO THEIR **POTENTIAL**
AND **GRATEFUL** FOR THEIR LESSONS

IN EVERY SITUATION YOU HAVE THE CHOICE WHETHER TO SEE

A STUMBLING BLOCK
OR
A STEPPING STONE

WHAT WILL YOU CHOOSE?

Don't **PUT THE NEEDS OF OTHERS BEFORE YOUR OWN!**

LIKE A BATTERY PACK, YOU MUST CHARGE YOURSELF BEFORE YOU CAN CHARGE OTHERS

THIS GOES AGAINST ONE OF YOUR CORE BELIEFS, BUT THE TRUTH IS

BY TAKING CARE OF YOUSELF, YOU'LL BE ABLE TO HELP OTHERS MORE

THE TEACHER *DOESN'T* APPEAR~~S~~ WHEN THE STUDENT IS READY

The teacher is *always* there!

BUT THE STUDENT WON'T NOTICE UNTIL THE STUDENT IS READY

STAY ALERT • KEEP AN OPEN MIND

DON'T LET YOUR EMOTIONS KEEP YOU FROM SEEING THE OPPORTUNITIES FOR GROWTH. ASK YOURSELF:

what is this trying to teach me?

NO GOOFING OFF!

GOOFiNG OFF
iS ONE OF THE BEST WAYS TO SPEND YOUR TIME

DON'T WAiT FOR THE WEEKEND
DON'T WAiT FOR THE ALCOHOL
DON'T WAiT TiLL YOU'RE ALONE

STOP BEiNG THE PERSON "THEY" EXPECT YOU TO BE

AND BE THE goofball THAT YOUR ARE!

LIFE IS ~~COMPLICATED~~ SIMPLE

SIMPLY
LIVE AUTHENTICALLY
BY
SHINING YOUR LIGHT
LOVING YOURSELF
HELPING OTHERS
HAVING FUN
BEING KIND

DON'T SET OUT TO CHANGE THE WORLD

Change Worlds
BY LIVING LIFE AS YOUR AUTHENTIC SELF!

BY DOING THIS, YOU INSPIRE OTHERS TO DO THE SAME
THEN SIMPLY SIT BACK AND ENJOY THE MAGIC UNFOLDING
AS THEY FINALLY FEEL FREE TO RELEASE THE LIGHT FROM
WITHIN AND LIVE THE LIFE THEY CAME HERE TO LIVE

WHY CHANGE THE WORLD WHEN YOU CAN
Change Worlds?

YOU ARE ^Not LOST!
Nor have you ever been,
Nor will you ever be!

LIFE IS A BEAUTIFUL
ADVENTURE!
THIS IS THE
TIME, SPACE & SETTING
IN WHICH YOU WERE MEANT TO BE
SO RELAX
TAKE A DEEP BREATH
AND MAKE YOUR NEXT MOVE

www.ingramcontent.com/pod-product-compliance
Lightning Source LLC
Chambersburg PA
CBHW061149070526
44584CB00034B/4468